Amazing
Origami

Kunihiko Kasahara

Sterling Publishing Co., Inc.
New York

Acknowledgments

A heartfelt thank-you to my friends Marieke de Hoop, Paulo Mulatinho and his wife Silke Schroeder, and to Michiko Yoshihara. They all encouraged me to write this book and supported me in every possible way. I have made a great many wonderful friends throughout the world thanks to origami, and for that, too, I am grateful.

Photography: Klaus Lipa, Diedorf bei Augsburg, Germany
Interior layout: Michael Stiehl, Leipzig, Germany

Library of Congress Cataloging-in-Publication Data

Kasahara, Kunihiko, 1941–
    [Origami--figürlich und geometrisch. English]
    Amazing origami / Kunihiko Kasahara.
      p. cm.
    ISBN 0-8069-5821-9
    1. Origami. I. Title.

   TT870 .K2815 2001
   736'.982--dc21

               00-053193

10 9 8 7 6 5 4 3 2 1

First paperback edition published in 2002 by
Sterling Publishing Company, Inc.
387 Park Avenue South, New York, N.Y. 10016
First published in Germany and © 2000 by Augustus Verlag
in der Weltbild Ratgeber Verlage GmbH & Co. KG
under the title *Origami — figürlich und geometrisch*
English translation © 2001 by Sterling Publishing Co., Inc.
Distributed in Canada by Sterling Publishing
C/o Canadian Manda Group, One Atlantic Avenue, Suite 105
Toronto, Ontario, Canada M6K 3E7
Distributed in Great Britain and Europe by Chris Lloyd at Orca Book
Services, Stanley House, Fleets Lane, Poole BH15 3AJ, England.
Distributed in Australia by Capricorn Link (Australia) Pty. Ltd.
P.O. Box 704, Windsor, NSW 2756 Australia
Printed in China
All rights reserved

Sterling ISBN 0-8069-5821-9 Hardcover
                0-8069-7420-6 Paperback

Contents

Preface

We start off with a square piece of paper. If we fold it according to origami rules, we place a corner on top of another corner, one edge on top of another. We are really applying mathematical principles for dividing segments, angles and areas into equal parts.

Friedrich Wilhelm August Froebel (1782 - 1852), a German teacher, recognized the connection between origami and geometry. He found origami a very useful teaching aid, which he used in a playful manner to help children develop an interest in and understanding of geometry. I myself am neither a teacher nor a mathematician, but during the course of my 40-year work with origami, I have come to greatly appreciate his ideas.

About 150 years have passed since Froebel taught, and origami has grown since then by leaps and bounds. I am filled with pride and joy that I have been given the opportunity to publish a book based on Froebel's ideas, which will hopefully give them renewed recognition. I sincerely hope that this joy will convey itself to the readers of my book.

What Is Origami?

What is origami? This question has kept me occupied for 20 years. I am sure this has happened to you as well: it is often very difficult to clearly explain a simple matter with which you are very familiar. I have searched for an answer to my question in many encyclopedias and origami books, but unfortunately have never found a satisfying definition. All explanations, in my view, only touch part of what origami is and therefore do not do justice to its wide range of characteristics and possibilities.

For me, the answer can be found in a kind of symbiosis, the coming together of different aspects that make up the whole. My own personal definition of origami is as follows: Origami is a traditional game of folding paper that unites sculptural esthetic aspects with functional and geometric-mathematical principles. Origami opens up interesting possibilities for people of all ages, regardless of sex, nationality, or language. With respect to my definition of origami as a game, I have heard several contrasting opinions. Many experts seem to think that calling it a game belittles the value of origami. For me, however, the playful aspect is essential to origami and by no means takes away from its significance. Play and a playful mindset create joy and enthusiasm, without which all arts and sciences would be empty.

Origami Symbols

Below are the most important origami symbols. They are used all over the world, and form the basis of the folding instructions in this book.

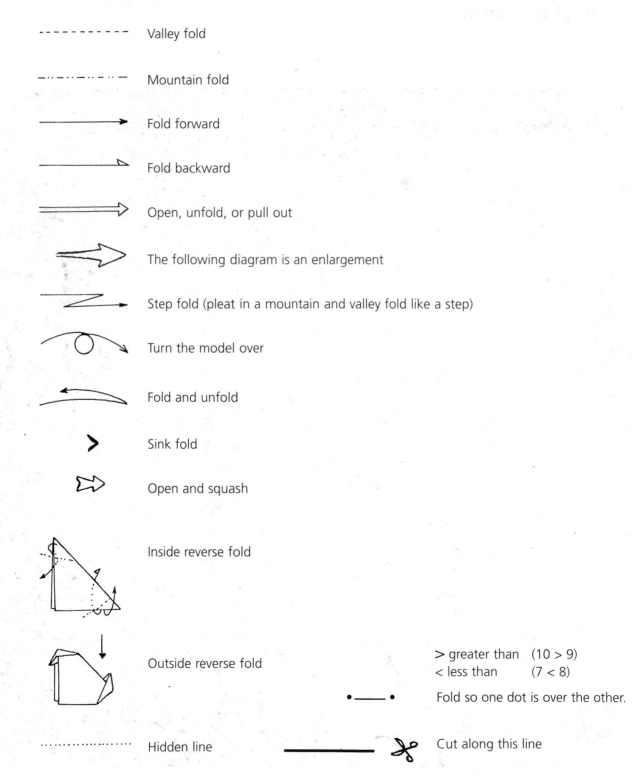

------------ Valley fold

—·—·—·— Mountain fold

———————→ Fold forward

———————▷ Fold backward

═══════⇒ Open, unfold, or pull out

The following diagram is an enlargement

Step fold (pleat in a mountain and valley fold like a step)

Turn the model over

Fold and unfold

> Sink fold

Open and squash

Inside reverse fold

Outside reverse fold

> greater than   (10 > 9)
< less than   (7 < 8)

•——• Fold so one dot is over the other.

················· Hidden line

——————✂ Cut along this line

Paper

I have used simple, square origami papers for all the models shown in this book. Where an oblong or a polygonal shape is needed, I will show how to make this from a square piece of paper.

The Link Between Esthetics and Geometry

"Mathematics is the noblest of sciences, the queen of sciences." How often 1 have heard remarks like this! 1 developed a longing for mathematics and envied mathematicians. 1 wanted nothing more than to enjoy the beauty of math myself.

Origami made it possible for me to realize this dream. What is more, 1 am very proud that origami makes it possible to revive figures that have been proven nonconstructible by Euclidean means and therefore disappeared — mathematical tables sometimes don't even list them.

For instance, the two figures on the right show two regular polygons. It is impossible to construct a regular 11-sided polygon (undecagon) using nothing but a compass and a ruler. The regular 17-sided polygon (heptadecagon) can be constructed with the help of a compass and a ruler, but this is rather complicated. With origami, it is not very difficult to construct both these figures. What was considered impossible suddenly becomes possible.

Origami creates a perfect union of esthetics and geometry, feelings and reasoning. That's what this book is all about.

Regular 11-Sided Polygon (Undecagon)
It is impossible to construct a regular undecagon using a compass and a ruler. This book, for the first time ever, explains a simple method of constructing this figure (see p. 39).

Regular 17-Sided Polygon (Heptadecagon)
The mathematician and astronomer Carl Friedrich Gauss (1777 – 1855) proved that it is possible to construct a regular 17-sided polygon, using a compass and a ruler. Have you ever tried to construct one? If so, you will know how difficult it is. Origami, however, makes it easy.

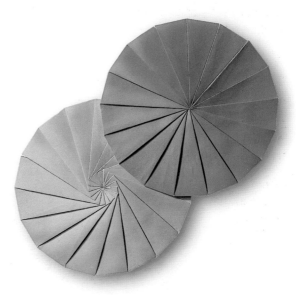

Kazuo Haga is a biologist and a pioneer of the new school of origami. His theorem is an important basis for origami mathematics.

Haga's Theorem
Triangles a, b and c are similar to each other. Their sides have the same ratios, 3 : 4 : 5.

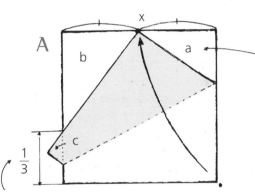

Changing the position of point x will result in different ratios.

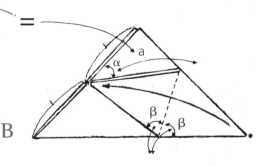

At first glance, there seems to be no connection between diagram A and diagram B. However, both are based on the same theorem and on a very similar way of folding.

Diagrams B and C appear to be the same, but have in fact very different meanings.

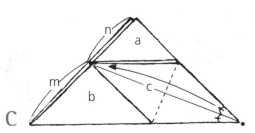

On page 28, you will find a practical method for the approximate construction of a regular pentagon, following the American tradition.

This approximation can be proven with the help of Haga's theorem. According to Haga, triangle a is a 3 : 4 : 5 triangle.
$\tan \alpha = 3/4$. From this it follows that:
$\alpha = 36.869° \approx 36°$
$\beta \approx 72° = 360°/5$

Here, the divider is formed by the angle bisector. Triangle c is an isosceles triangle and triangles a and b are similar isosceles triangles. The areas of a and b have the ratio of 1 : 2. It then follows that:
$n : m = 1 : \sqrt{2}$

Dividing Areas in Half

If you fold a square diagonally, you will create a right isosceles triangle. We will take its area to be 1. Now continue to halve this triangle again and again by placing the acute angles on top of each other, ten times in total (see diagrams 1 through 7).

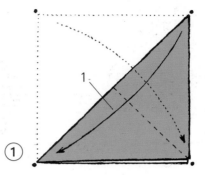

$$1 \cdot \frac{1}{2} = \frac{1}{2^1}$$

$$\frac{1}{2} \cdot \frac{1}{2} = \frac{1}{4} = \frac{1}{2^2}$$

$$\frac{1}{4} \cdot \frac{1}{2} = \frac{1}{8} = \frac{1}{2^3}$$

$$\frac{1}{8} \cdot \frac{1}{2} = \frac{1}{16} = \frac{1}{2^4}$$

$$\vdots$$

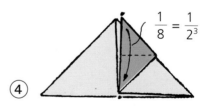

The area of the last and smallest triangle is $1/2^{10}$ or $1/1024$. If we were to halve and fold over the triangles an infinite number of times and add up the areas of all the triangles thus created, the sum of all the sub-triangles would result in the original triangle with the area 1. Expressed in a formula, this would look as follows:

$$1/2 + 1/2^2 + 1/2^3 + 1/2^4 + 1/2^5 + \ldots 1/2^n + \ldots = 1$$

The Indian mathematician T. Sundara Row, who lived about a hundred years after Froebel, first introduced this principle of clarifying complex mathematical relationships in a simple manner by using origami.

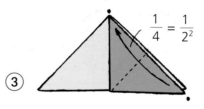

However, mathematical discoveries aren't the only relevant point. It is also important to create an esthetically pleasing object in the process. Take a look at the spiral structure on page 11, for example.

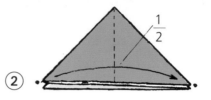

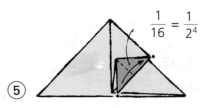

Spiral Shape

The shape that is produced after halving the triangle ten times (see diagram 7) is an esthetically pleasing object. However, if you unfold it again and change the orientation of the three folds along sides a and b (turn mountain folds into valley folds), you will turn the two-dimensional, flat shape into a fascinating, plastic spiral shape.

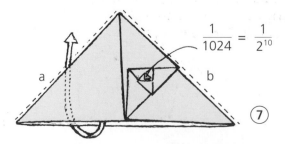

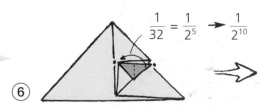

$$\frac{1}{32} = \frac{1}{2^5} \rightarrow \frac{1}{2^{10}}$$

$$\frac{1}{1024} = \frac{1}{2^{10}}$$

a

b

⑥

⑦

T. Sundara Row did not use quite the same method as demonstrated on pages 10 to 11. This method of halving the area of a right isosceles triangle was introduced by Jun Maekawa, of Japan. It is easier to understand than Row's idea of how to halve areas, shown in figure A. The idea is the same, but Maekawa's method is even simpler and must therefore be seen as progress. What is more, following Row's method, the square can only be halved about four times.

If we compare the two methods, it becomes obvious that both shapes have the same area (see figure B). This is easy to see, and was noted by Froebel.

Interestingly enough, origami paper usually has a white side and a colored side. If you consider figure B again and keep this in mind, you will realize that the colored areas (folded over the square) completely cover the white area. And so it is proven, very simply and clearly, that if the area of the original square is taken to be 1, the areas of the two shapes in figure B are half of the area of the square, or 1/2.

Froebel, too, discussed these mathematical principles and got as far as figure B, but never arrived at figure D on page 13.

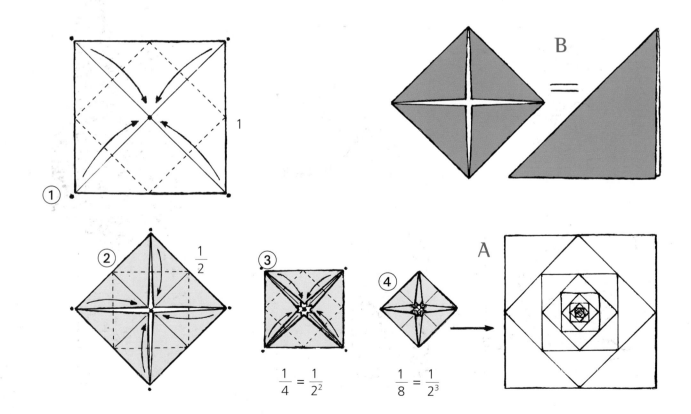

A Monument to Froebel

The Froebel Museum is located in Bad Blankenburg in Thuringia, Germany. Up on a hill, where Froebel often came to think and where he enjoyed an unhindered view over the pretty spa town, there now stands a monument to Froebel.

It is a stone sculpture which consists of a cube, a cylinder and a sphere. Seen from the side, the cube and the cylinder have the same square outline. Seen from above, the sphere and the cylinder look like circles (see diagram C).

From certain points of view, different shapes appear to be the same. Different figures have, for example, the same area. With this as a starting point, we will discover that there are more possibilities for folding a square so that the white area is covered exactly by the colored area (see figure D below). Please try to remember these, as there is an interesting puzzle that I would like to introduce to you later (see page 44).

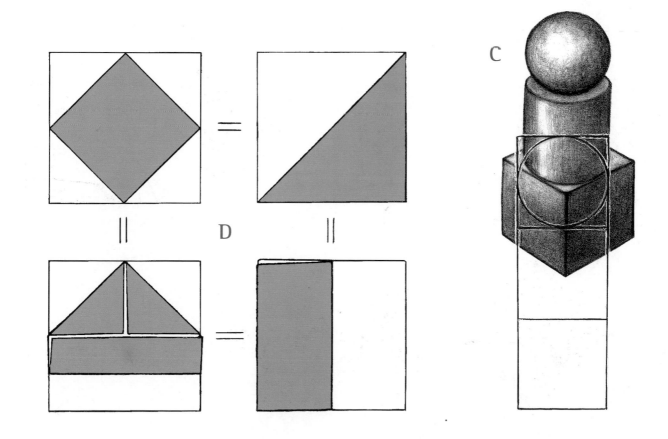

Dividing Angles in Half

The previous pages discussed dividing areas in half. We will now move on to dividing angles in half. Follow the step-by-step instructions to fold the Crow and Grass. Then we will examine the completed figures with respect to the angles that were created and what this means in a mathematical context. You will learn a lot of interesting facts about angles. Finally, you will see an example concerning the division of angles into three parts (page 16).

Roulette

(by Paolo Bascetta)

I discovered this figure also, and introduced it at the same time in Japan. The world is full of coincidences!

③

④

②

①

8 x

Here, the paper is folded in the opposite direction from the way it is folded for Grass.

This first step of Roulette corresponds to step 3 in folding Grass.

Tuck 2nd module (right) into the 1st; fold sides of 1st around 2nd.

Fold and add the remaining 6 modules the same way.

⑤

⑥

⑦

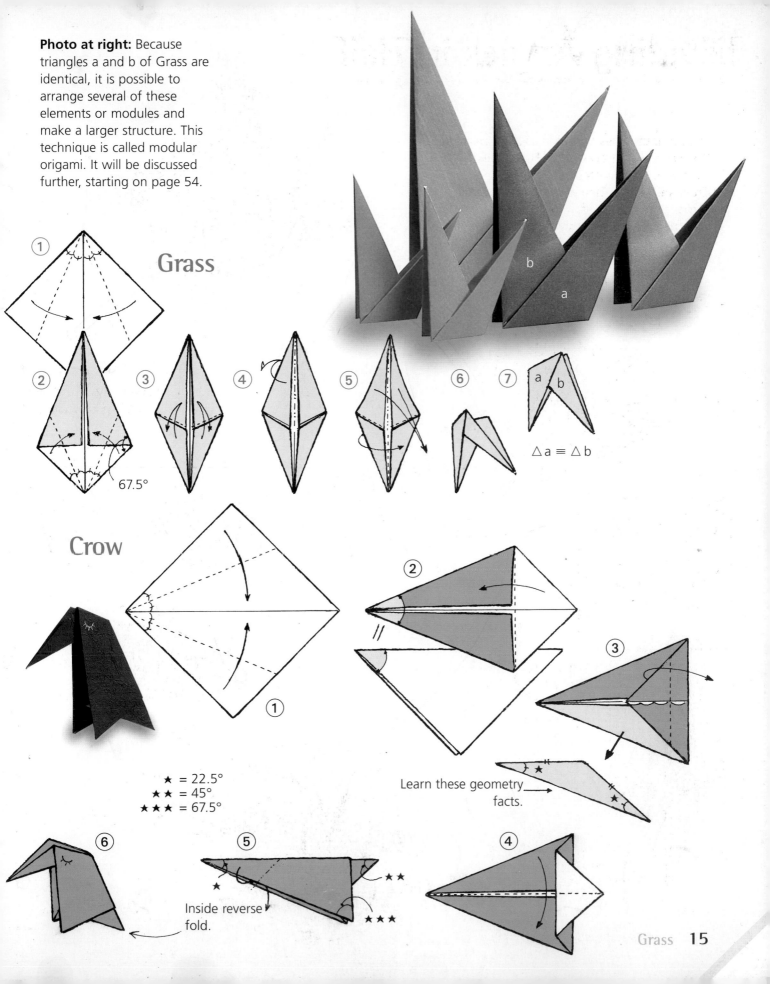

Photo at right: Because triangles a and b of Grass are identical, it is possible to arrange several of these elements or modules and make a larger structure. This technique is called modular origami. It will be discussed further, starting on page 54.

Grass

① ② ③ ④ ⑤ ⑥ ⑦

67.5°

a   b

△a ≡ △b

Crow

①

②

③

Learn these geometry facts.

★ = 22.5°
★★ = 45°
★★★ = 67.5°

⑥ ⑤ ④

Inside reverse fold.

Dividing Angles in Thirds

In order to fold this model, we will need equilateral triangles. To create them, you will need to fold 60° angles from the origami square. Since 60° is two-thirds of a right angle (90°), the first step is to divide a right angle into three parts.

Star of David

Blow gently through a straw onto the Star and it will start to spin.

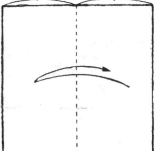

①

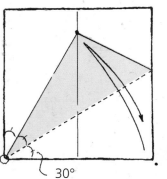

②

30°

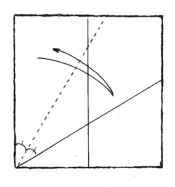

③

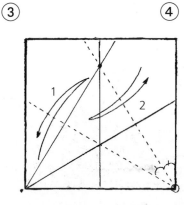

④

Fold the right side the same way as the left side.

⑤

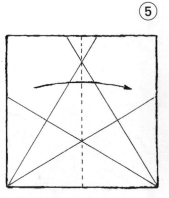

If you wish to fold the Star of David in just one color, use the paper folded double.

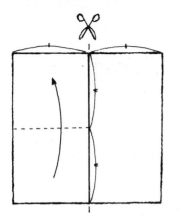

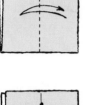

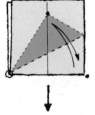

Continue with step 3.

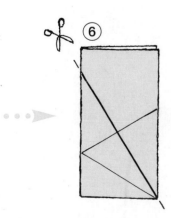

The finished model

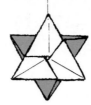

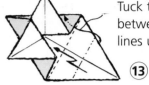

If you assemble the Star the opposite way, the direction of spin will change.

Fold in the order given.

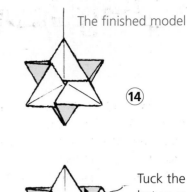

⑭

Tuck the part between the lines under.

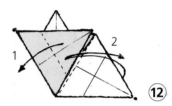

⑬

1

2

⑫

1

⑪

2

Characteristics of an equilateral triangle

Learn these characteristics well:

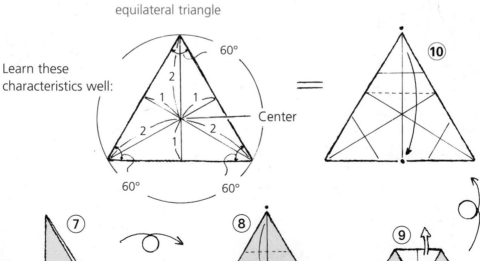

60°

2

1   1

2   2

Center

1

60°   60°

=

⑩

⑥

⑦

⑧

⑨

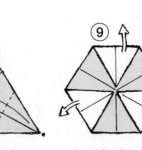

Equilateral triangle

Regular hexagon

Regular Hexagon

On pages 16 and 17, you learned the folding technique for an equilateral triangle. From this, you can easily fold a regular hexagon (see figure E); however, the resulting hexagon will be quite small.

Let's try to discover how we can use an origami square to create as large a hexagon as possible. You can then use this to fold the beautiful Vase shown on page 19.

Equilateral triangle and regular hexagon.

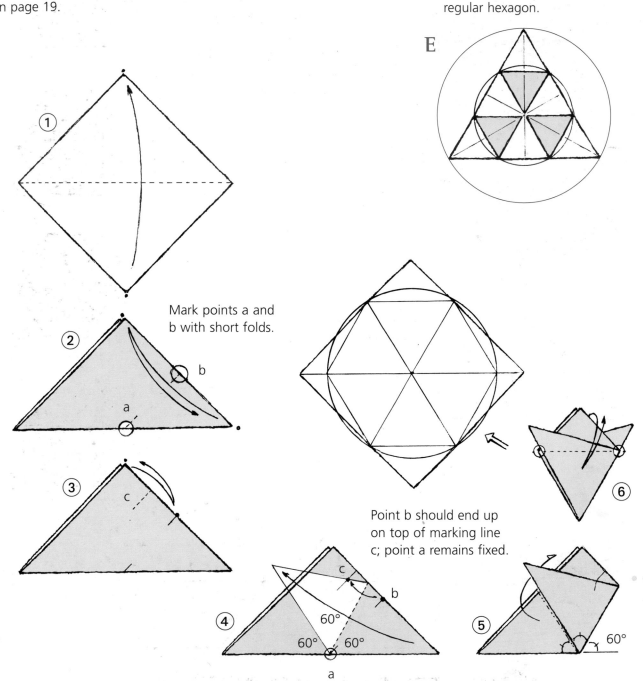

Mark points a and b with short folds.

Point b should end up on top of marking line c; point a remains fixed.

Vase

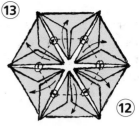

Prefold the border of the Vase's base.

Make the Vase by pushing out the side to raise it up, with one finger inside the Vase and another pressing from the outside.

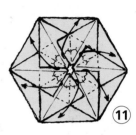

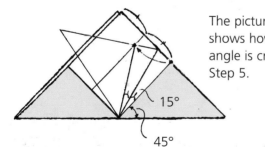

The picture at left shows how the 60° angle is created in Step 5.

15°

45°

Why not try to fold this unusual vase from other regular polygons?

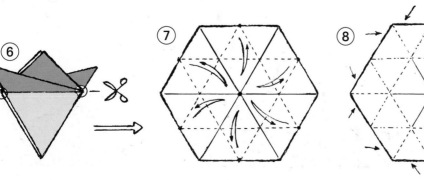

Regular 12-Sided Polygon

Next we'll fold a regular 12-sided polygon (dodecagon).

Use this form to fold a Vase, following the method shown for the hexagon on the previous pages.

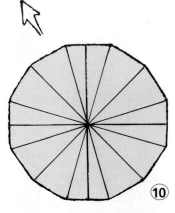

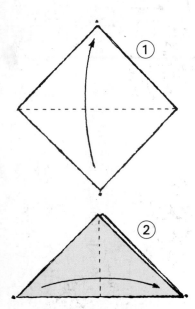

①

②

③

④

Mark only the top layer of paper with a short marking line.

90° / 3 = 30°, dividing the right angle into 3 parts, as was shown for the Star of David.

⑩

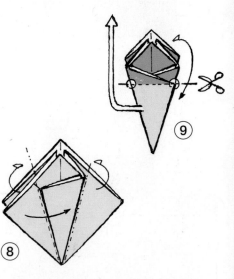

⑨

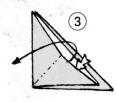

⑤

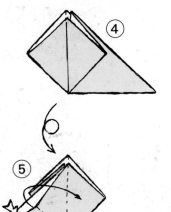

⑥

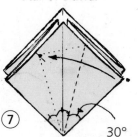

⑦   30°

⑧

Twelve-Winged Spinning Top

This example shows how we can create a figure with twelve corners from a square piece of paper. The Spinning Top will start to turn if you blow on it from above.

Start with the colored side of the paper up and fold the area into 16 equal-sized squares, in the order shown.

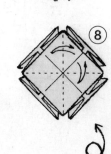

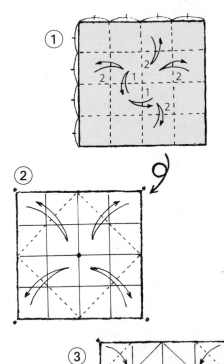

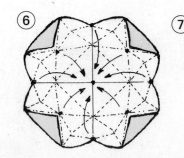

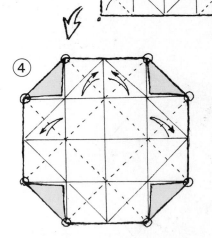

Change those parts of the valley folds marked with circles into mountain folds; then fold up the shape.

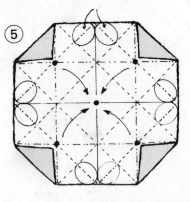

Dividing Segments Into Parts

Halving a segment, dividing it into two equal parts, is the simplest way of dividing and the most basic origami folding action. However, by using this simple method, we can actually also divide a segment into three, five or seven equal parts. This remarkable and astonishing folding method was developed by Mr. Shuzo Fujimoto, a teacher at a Japanese grammar school who has greatly enriched the world of origami with his works.

Diagrams F-1 to F-3 show his method of dividing. The first step always marks a random point on the paper's edge. In the steps that follow, further markings are made using a specific rhythm, whereby the new marking divides the segment left (A) or right (B) of the last marking. The new markings hit the desired points of division more accurately each time.

After only a few repeats, the desired point of division is marked as accurately as folding will allow. The only (minor) disadvantage of this method is that it leaves some undesired markings on the edge of the paper. If you want to avoid these little folds, it is best to use a folding template with the desired divisions. These templates are easily made. Figures G-1 and G-2 show how to use templates with a base 2 division to divide a segment into an odd number of equal-sized parts.

Figure H (page 23) shows an even simpler method of dividing a segment into three parts. This is not a mathematical method, and it is only suitable for division into three parts, but, with a little practice, it is quickly done and does not leave any undesirable markings.

Division by Iteration
(method of Shuzo Fujimoto)

F–1

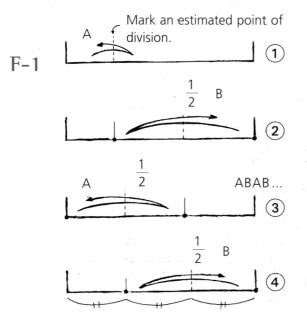

Folding rhythm for 3 equal parts: ABAB...

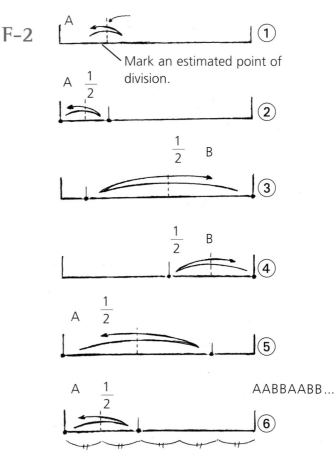

Folding rhythm for 5 equal parts: AABBAABB...

Mr. Fujimoto's method of division does not end with seven equal parts, and can be used to divide segments into 9, 11, 13, ... 91, 101, ... etc. equal parts. Can you work out the folding rhythms?

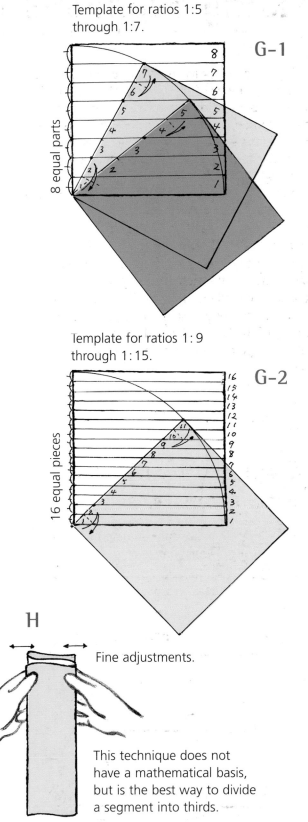

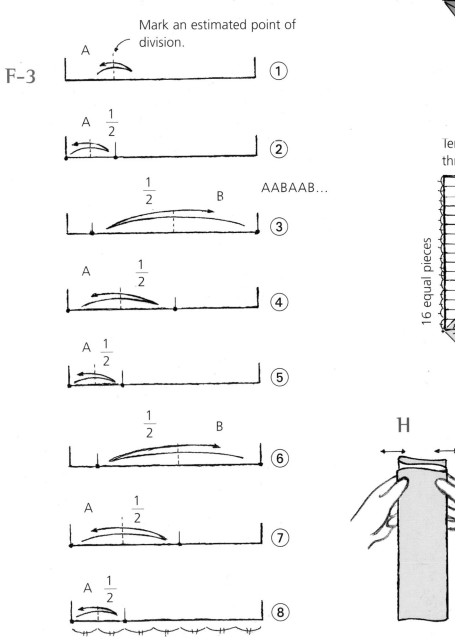

Mark an estimated point of division.

F-3

AABAAB...

H Fine adjustments.

This technique does not have a mathematical basis, but is the best way to divide a segment into thirds.

Folding rhythm for 7 equal parts: AABAAB...

Shooting Star
(method of Jun Maekawa)

By making this pretty Shooting Star, you can put into practice the method you have just learned for dividing segments into equal parts. As an example, we use Jun Maekawa's masterpiece (see page 25).

By changing the dividing factor, I was able to greatly simplify the folding pattern. The method I use here is based on division into twelve parts.

① Start by placing the paper face up with your chosen color for the finished Star showing; fold in 3 equal parts.

② Halve all three areas with valley folds and unfold.

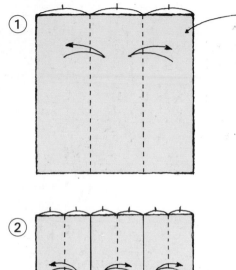

③ Divide each area further with valley folds and make mountain folds where shown, working towards the center.

④

⑤

⑥ You should end up with seven points.

⑦ Unfold and turn over.

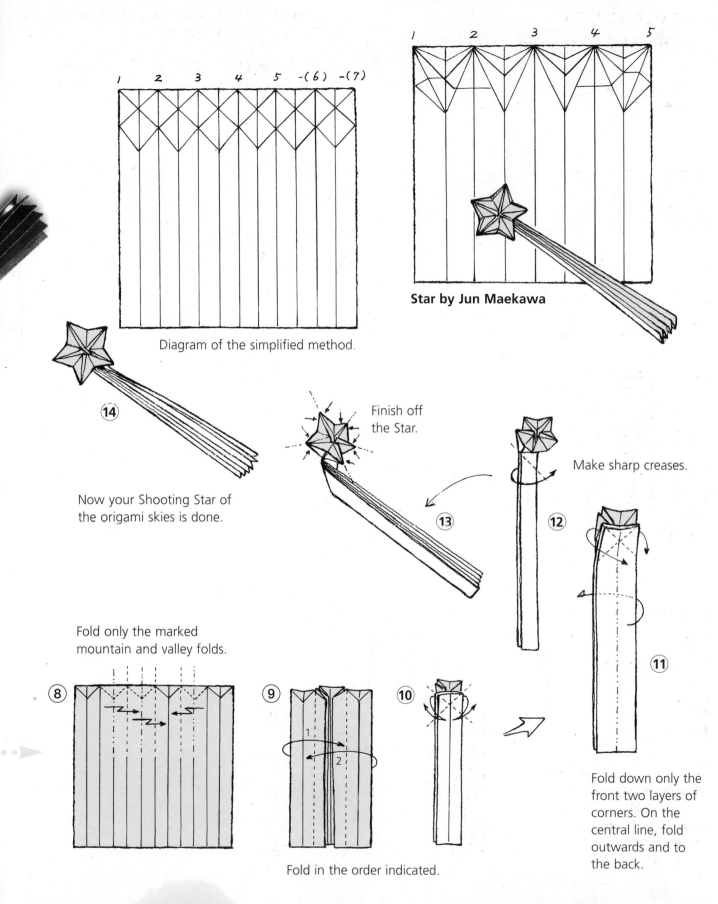

1 2 3 4 5 -(6) -(7)

Diagram of the simplified method.

1 2 3 4 5

Star by Jun Maekawa

⑭

Now your Shooting Star of the origami skies is done.

Finish off the Star.

⑬

Make sharp creases.

⑫

⑪

Fold only the marked mountain and valley folds.

⑧

⑨

1

2

Fold in the order indicated.

⑩

Fold down only the front two layers of corners. On the central line, fold outwards and to the back.

Regular Octagon

The regular octagon is easily made by repeated halving of angles. However, I would like to introduce you to a different technique here, called iso-area folding. This was invented by Toshikazu Kawasaki, a Japanese mathematician and prominent origami scholar.

You will get very impressive results if you use two pieces of paper of different colors, creating an embrace of the two surfaces. By folding further, you will produce a UFO.

UFO

Place two different-colored paper squares on top of each other, colored sides facing up. Fold.

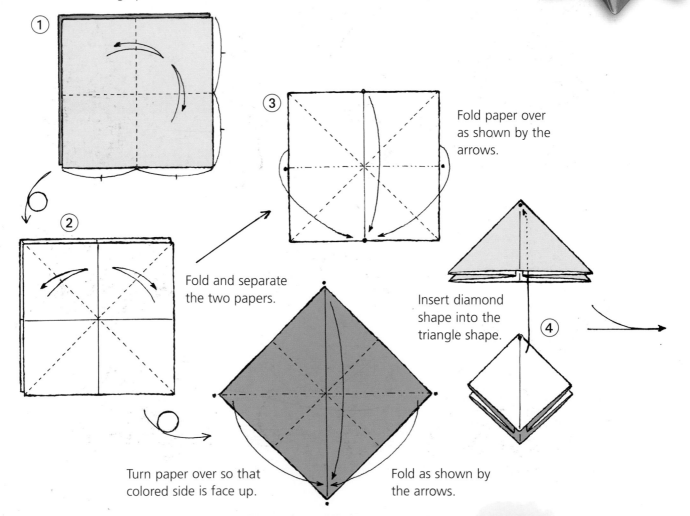

Fold and separate the two papers.

Fold paper over as shown by the arrows.

Insert diamond shape into the triangle shape.

Turn paper over so that colored side is face up.

Fold as shown by the arrows.

No matter how often the shape is turned, it remains the same, and that is what *iso-area* means. This shape could also represent a jelly-fish or a sea anemone.

Open and turn.

(18)

(17)

(16)

Make 4 inside reverse folds.

(15)

(14)

Open and turn.

The two layers of paper will hold together well.

(13)

Make 4 inside reverse folds.

(12)

(11)

(10)

45°

45°

45°

45°

Regular octagon.

(5)

Once you have understood this principle, you will be able to fold a regular octagon from a single sheet of paper.

(9)

(6)

(7)

Open out.

(8)

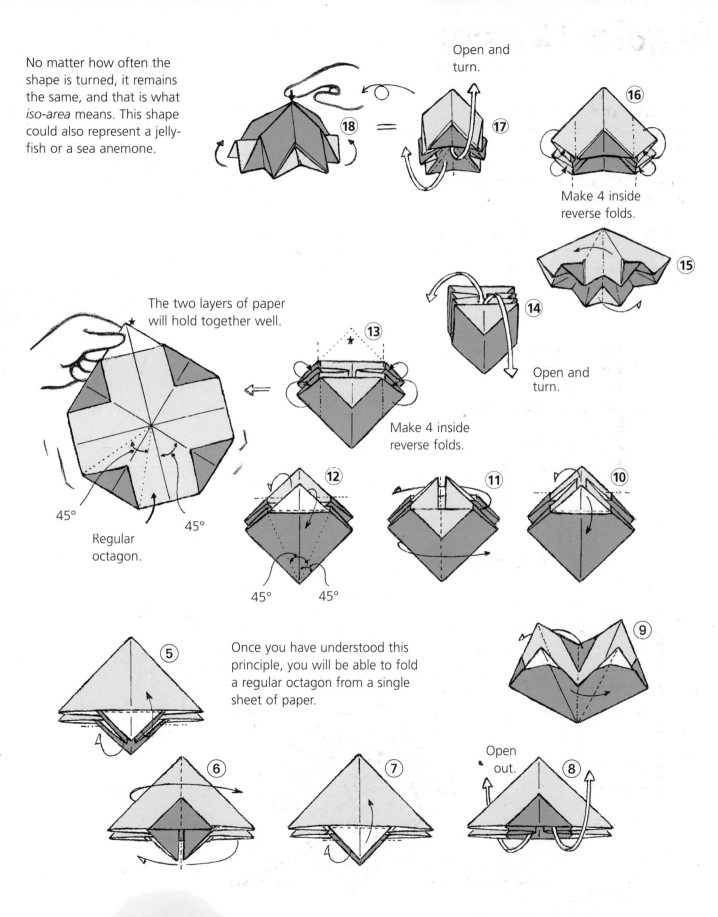

Regular Pentagon

Many blossoms have five petals; for example, *sakura* (the Japanese name for "cherry blossom," the symbol of Japan), *ume* (Japanese cherry blossom), *momo* (peach blossom), and *kikyo* (mountain bell). You can well imagine how difficult it is to fold five petals of equal size from a square of paper. This task might be a little easier with a pentagonal paper shape, but unfortunately it is also rather tricky to produce this.

The obvious answer is to divide the 360° angle at the center of the square by five (360° / 5 = 72°). But 72° cannot be folded as easily as 120° (for an equilateral triangle), 90° (for a square), 60° (to make a regular hexagon), 45° (for a regular octagon) or 30° (for a

regular dodecagon). Many people in the past have tried to fold a regular pentagon.

In the following, I will introduce two of several possible solutions, one according to Japanese tradition and one according to American tradition.

The error for the American method is -0.6%; for the Japanese method, +0.2%. Both deviations are smaller than the accuracy that can be achieved through folding, so both techniques are therefore handy methods of approximation.

American Method

This is a slightly easier folding technique, but it will result in a smaller pentagon (see diagram on page 29).

Japanese Method

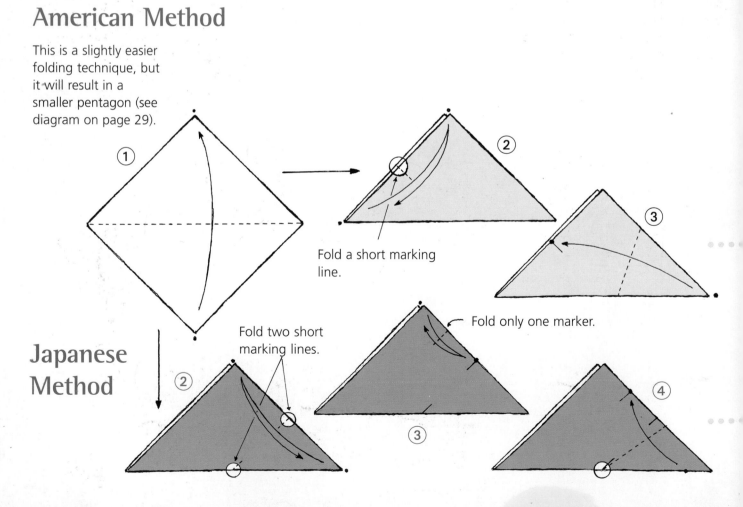

Fold a short marking line.

Fold two short marking lines.

Fold only one marker.

28   Regular Pentagon

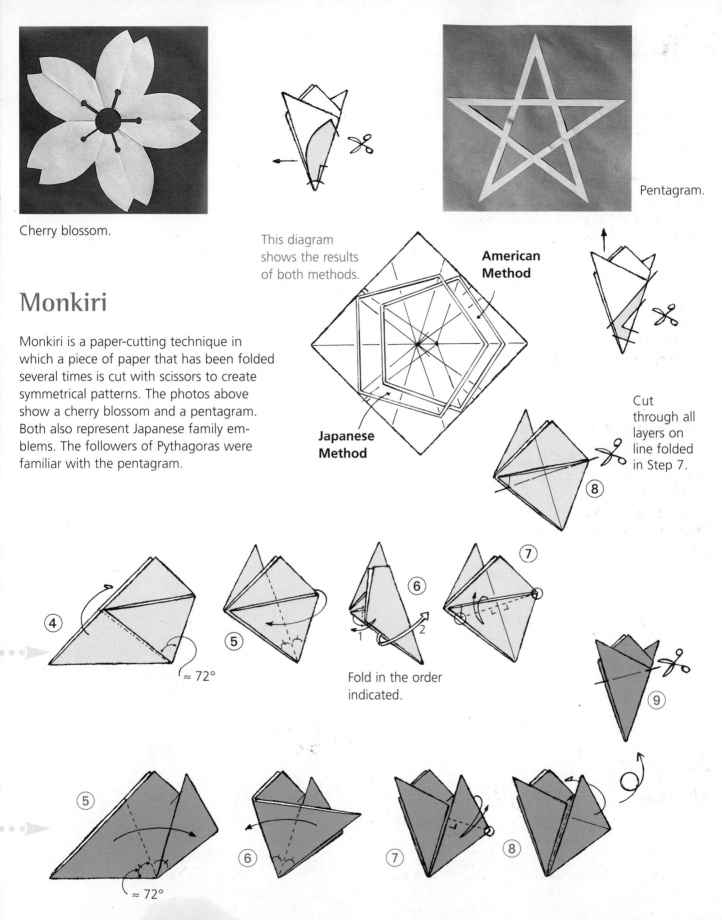

Cherry blossom.

Pentagram.

Monkiri

Monkiri is a paper-cutting technique in which a piece of paper that has been folded several times is cut with scissors to create symmetrical patterns. The photos above show a cherry blossom and a pentagram. Both also represent Japanese family emblems. The followers of Pythagoras were familiar with the pentagram.

This diagram shows the results of both methods.

American Method

Japanese Method

Cut through all layers on line folded in Step 7.

⑧

⑦

⑥

④ ≈ 72°

⑤

Fold in the order indicated.

⑨

⑤ ≈ 72°

⑥

⑦

⑧

Characteristics of the Regular Pentagon

Both pentagon-folding techniques result in only a very minor error for the central angle of the regular pentagon, compared to its exact theoretical value. I don't really like the term "error." If you try to divide 360° into five equal parts simply by folding, it is almost impossible to avoid errors. If we look at the characteristics of the regular pentagon from a different point of view, we will come across a link to the golden mean (see Diagram A).

Today, an exact regular pentagon is often constructed with the help of the rules of the golden section; how-ever, this is rather difficult to fold. I have discovered a simple method with which we can fold a drawing template for a regular pentagon, without theoretical error.

Editor's comment: Due to the thickness of the paper, errors cannot be avoided, even if you fold very accurately. Every error made during one folding step contributes to the overall error of the end result, so that many small, unavoidable folding errors accumulate

into a rather large error, even with methods that theoretically produce an exact result. Methods of approximation in practice often give a more accurate result than theoretically exact methods. Kasahara manages, through integration of the third dimension, to use a simple method to fold theoretically exact drawing templates for regular polygons that otherwise cannot be constructed following Euclidean methods, or can be done only with great difficulty.

A

Golden rectangle.

Regular pentagon.

$$L / \ell = \ell / 1$$
$$\downarrow$$
$$L / \ell = 2 / (\sqrt{5} - 1)$$
$$= (\sqrt{5} + 1) / 2$$

$1 < \ell$

Drawing Template for the Regular Pentagon

This regular pentagon is (theoretically) error-free.

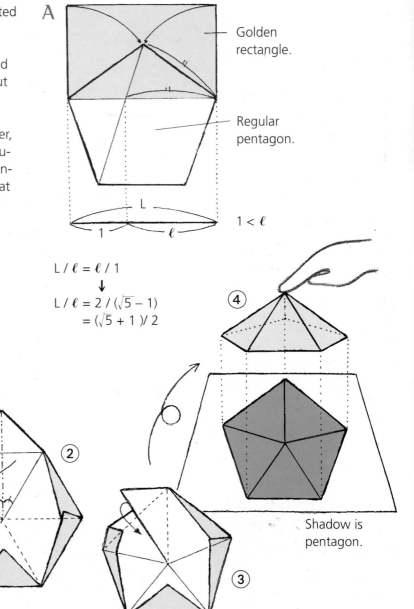

Regular hexagon (see page 18).

① ② ③ ④

Shadow is pentagon.

The Golden Rectangle

How can we divide the side of a square into fifths with only 1½ folds?

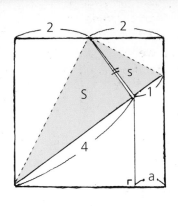

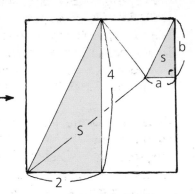

a = 1/5 the length of the side of a square

Proof:

Triangles S and s are similar. It then follows: a = 1/5 the length of the side of the square (note the ratio of the sides of triangles S and s).

b = 2/5 the length of the side of a square

Proof: Triangles S and s are similar.

a : b = 1 : 2. It then follows that b = 2/5 the length of the side of a square.

Fold in the order indicated.

Fold in the order indicated.

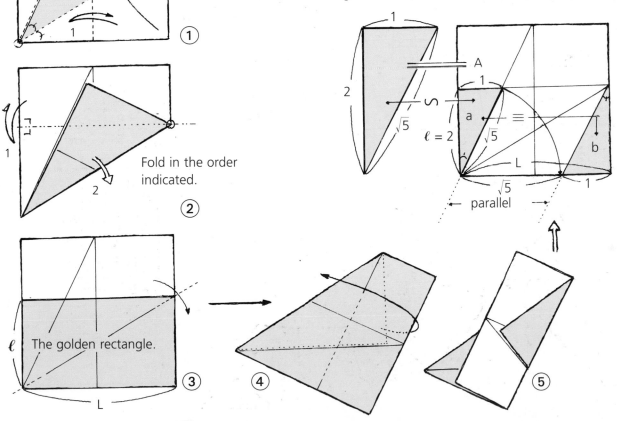

The golden rectangle.

⑥

Proof: Triangles A and a are similar. Triangles a and b are congruent. It then follows that:

$$\ell : L = 2 : (\sqrt{5} + 1)$$

The Impossible Becomes Possible

So far, we have constructed the equilateral triangle, the square (the basic shape for origami), the regular pentagon, hexagon, octagon and the dodecagon — six regular polygons in all. Geometry teaches that we cannot construct a regular 7-sided polygon (heptagon), 9-sided polygon (enneagon), or 11-sided polygon (undecagon) using a compass and a ruler.

It took mathematicians more than 2000 years to arrive at this conclusion! However, the following pages will prove that origami makes it possible to construct these shapes, without any tricks.

I was considering the definition of the regular polygon one day, when I experienced a breakthrough: Regular polygons are polygons whose sides are of equal length and whose interior angles are of equal size. *This definition does not state, however, that, in constructing these shapes, we are not allowed to use a point outside the plane of the polygon.* My solution is the base of a low equilateral polygonal pyramid.

Another Way to Fold a Regular Pentagon

This method is theoretically exact. Study this folding technique thoroughly, since you can use this new method to construct all other regular polygons.

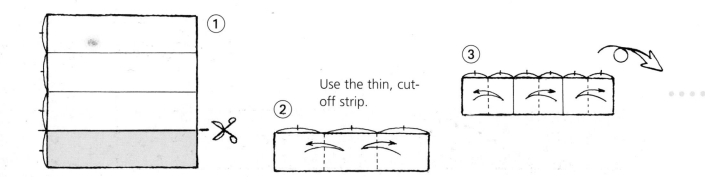

Use the thin, cut-off strip.

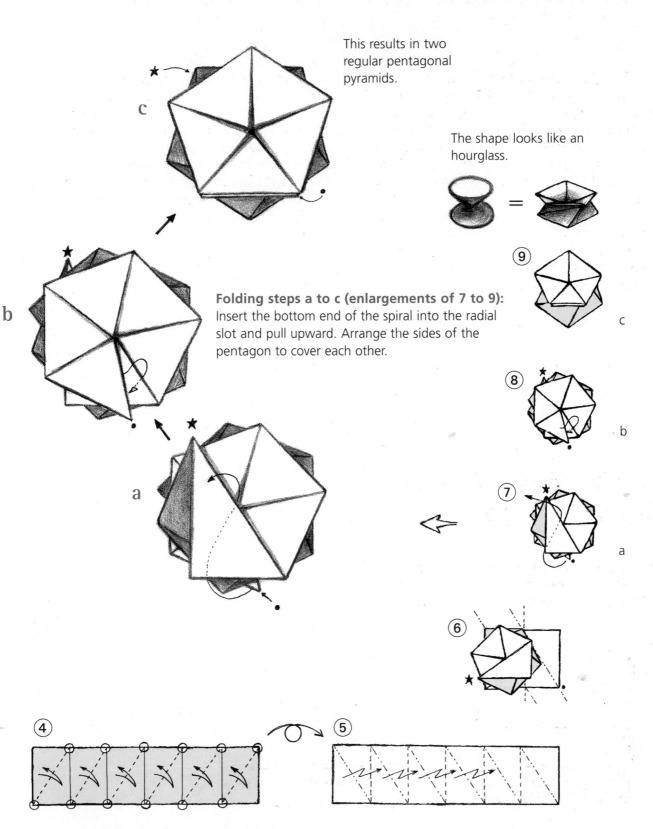

This results in two regular pentagonal pyramids.

The shape looks like an hourglass.

Folding steps a to c (enlargements of 7 to 9):
Insert the bottom end of the spiral into the radial slot and pull upward. Arrange the sides of the pentagon to cover each other.

Our first attempt with the new method.

Compass Folding

On the previous pages, you got to know a technique that allows you to fold two regular pentagonal pyramids in a simple manner, but with a mathematically accurate result. If we take a closer look at this technique (see diagram A below), we will find that we have actually drawn a circle that has its center at the center of one of the six rectangles, i.e., at the center of its diagonals. This folding technique therefore works like a drawing compass.

If you want to fold a regular pentagon instead of the regular pentagonal pyramid, the size of angle α has to be 54°. The measure of the angle can be

calculated as shown in diagram B on the opposite page. Through a number of preparatory folds (see figures 1 to 4), we can initially determine the measure of angle α and consequently the correct ratio of length to width of the rectangles.

As with the regular pentagonal pyramid, we will again create two regular pentagons. To get this, unfold the finished pentagon, cut the strip of paper in half lengthwise, and fold both pieces together again along the folding lines (see figures 7 to 9).

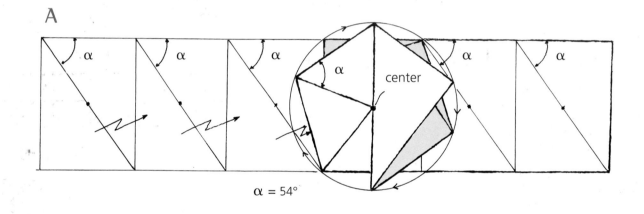

A

α = 54°

Fold in the order indicated.

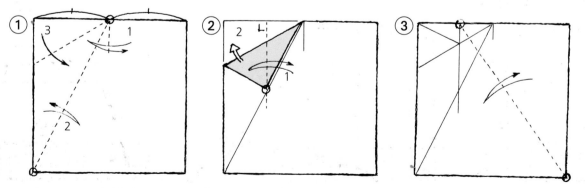

Preparatory folds for α ≈ 54° (α = 54.11...°).

Equilateral Triangle and Square

Using the same folding technique, you can also fold an equilateral triangle and a square.

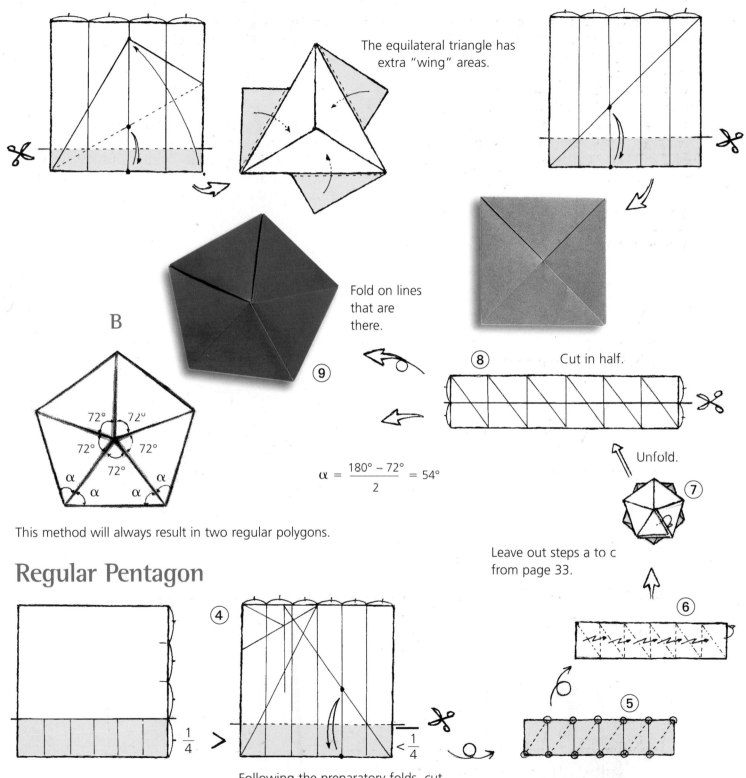

The equilateral triangle has extra "wing" areas.

Fold on lines that are there.

⑨

B

72° 72°
72° 72°
72°
α   α
α   α   α

$$\alpha = \frac{180° - 72°}{2} = 54°$$

This method will always result in two regular polygons.

⑧ Cut in half.

Unfold.

⑦

Leave out steps a to c from page 33.

⑥

⑤

Regular Pentagon

④

$\frac{1}{4}$ > < $\frac{1}{4}$

Following the preparatory folds, cut strip and fold into 6 equal rectangles.

Going Farther

Now that you are familiar with compass folding, you can apply this technique to the regular hexagon and the regular octagon. I have already given the templates required for division into seven and nine equal parts on page 23.

Afterwards, we will bravely confront the challenge of folding the regular heptagon, which cannot be constructed using a compass and a ruler. To construct a figure that up to now could not be constructed, we have to embrace a new way of thinking and confront the problem with imagination, in a playful manner. One solution, in

the shape of a regular heptagonal pyramid, already exists (see page 37). Well, yes, it's a pyramid — isn't that good enough for you? Then you might want to have a look at pages 38 to 39.

Editor's comment: When we speak of regular polygons that cannot be constructed mathematically, we always refer to the fact that they cannot be constructed using Euclidean means, i.e., using only a compass and a ruler. This does not mean that there aren't methods of construction using additional means that enable us to construct these. Origami is just one of the additional means of non-Euclidean construction, but by no means the only one.

Regular Hexagon

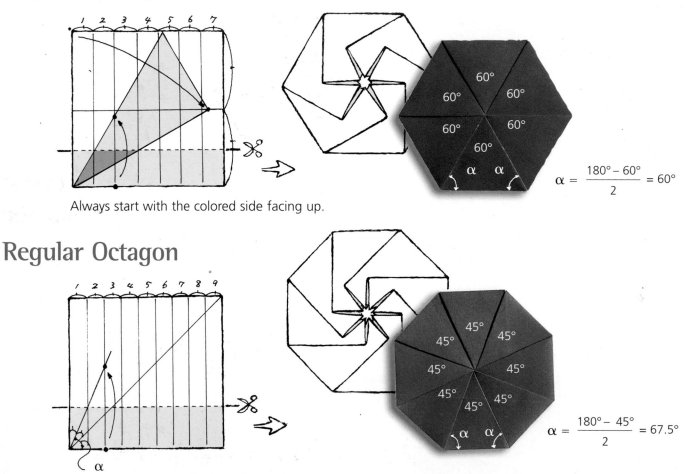

Always start with the colored side facing up.

$$\alpha = \frac{180° - 60°}{2} = 60°$$

Regular Octagon

$$\alpha = \frac{180° - 45°}{2} = 67.5°$$

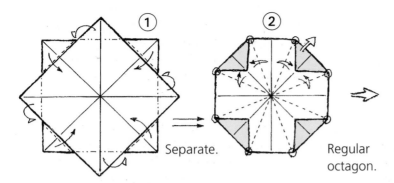

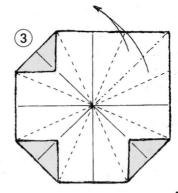

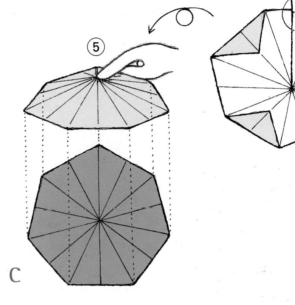

① ② Separate. Regular octagon. ③

For folding method, see page 36.

Regular Heptagonal (7-Sided) Pyramid

Calculating angle α

The triangles that result from connecting the center of a polygon with its corners are isosceles triangles, with two equal angles α and a central angle a.

Euclid's theorem (see page 43) applies to all triangles. It states that the sum of the interior angles of a triangle equals 180°. Angle α can then be calculated as follows:

$$\alpha = \frac{180° - a}{2}$$

C

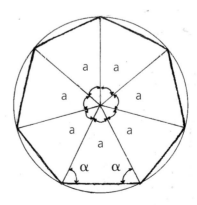

Regular Heptagon

$$a = \frac{360°}{7} = 51.428571°\ldots$$

$$\alpha = \frac{180° - a}{2} = \frac{450°}{7} = 64.285714°\ldots$$

The Answer Lies in Between

The regular hexagon and the regular octagon have already become reality thanks to the new compass folding technique. And we can be sure that the base angle of the determining triangle for the regular heptagon lies somewhere between the values of that of the hexagon and the octagon, as does the side ratio of the paper strip used for folding it.

On the other hand, the regular heptagon is no longer a total stranger, because we have already found a solution, although its "center" is not on the same plane as the heptagon itself.

I tried to create the necessary paper strip for the regular heptagon by dividing a square in 4 parts. However, this resulted in a heptagon with a hole in the middle. In diagram D (opposite page), points R6 and R8 are already marked. We have already constructed these to determine the width of the paper strips used for the regular hexagon and the regular octagon. Point R7, which determines the width of the paper strip for the regular heptagon, lies somewhere in between. The center of the segment R6 – R8 is a useful approximation for R7.

In practice, it is sufficient (due to paper thickness, etc.) if we fold the edge of the square just slightly over the central line, in order to create the paper strip required for a couple of beautiful regular heptagons.

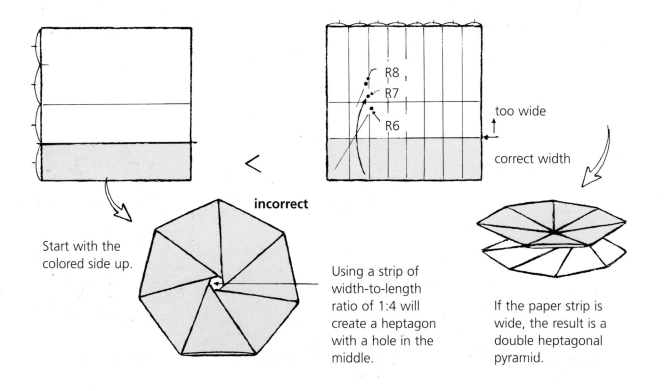

incorrect

Start with the colored side up.

Using a strip of width-to-length ratio of 1:4 will create a heptagon with a hole in the middle.

too wide

correct width

If the paper strip is wide, the result is a double heptagonal pyramid.

The determining point for the regular heptagon lies between the determining points for the regular hexagon and the regular octagon, just above the central line of the square.

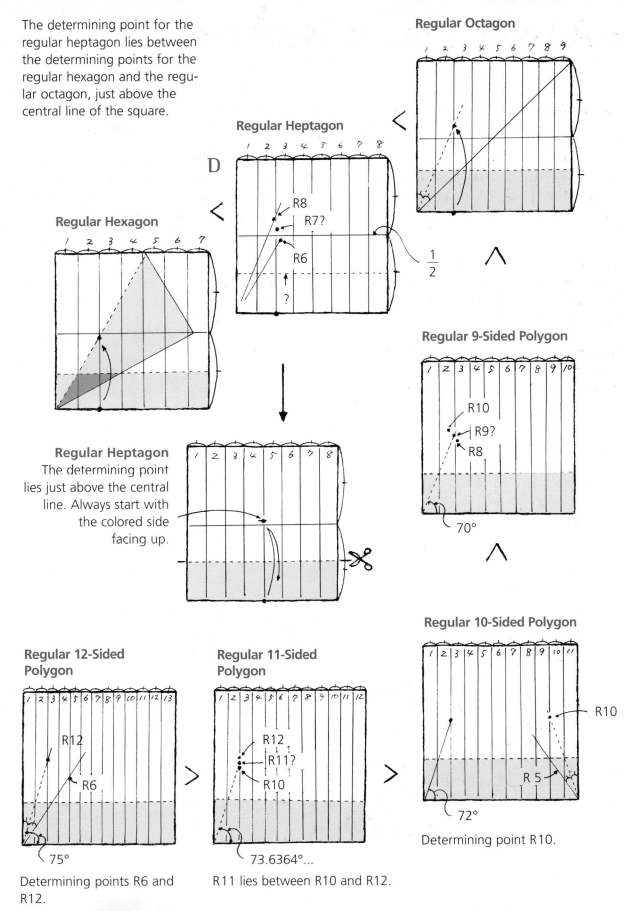

Regular Octagon

D

Regular Heptagon

R8
R7?
R6
?

$\frac{1}{2}$

Regular Hexagon

Regular Heptagon
The determining point lies just above the central line. Always start with the colored side facing up.

Regular 9-Sided Polygon

R10
R9?
R8

70°

Regular 12-Sided Polygon

R12
R6

75°

Determining points R6 and R12.

Regular 11-Sided Polygon

R12
R11?
R10

73.6364°...

R11 lies between R10 and R12.

Regular 10-Sided Polygon

R10
R5

72°

Determining point R10.

More "Nonconstructible" Shapes

If you have ever tried to put the regular pentagon on paper, or the regular 17-sided polygon (heptadecagon), proven to be constructible by Carl Friedrich Gauss (1777 – 1855), then you will know how difficult this is, using only a compass and a ruler. The regular pentagon's construction can be traced back to Pythagoras (around 570 – 497/96 B.C.).

With origami, however, you will do both very easily. The shapes that cannot be constructed using Euclidean means have become reality with the folding technique introduced earlier, and the end result is beautiful to look at. Therefore don't stop now, but keep folding more shapes following the same principle.

Regular 16-Sided Polygon

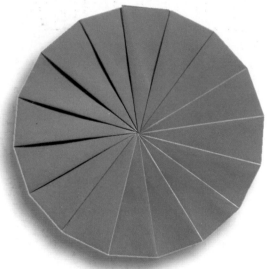

Regular 17-Sided Polygon

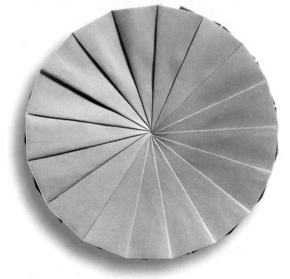

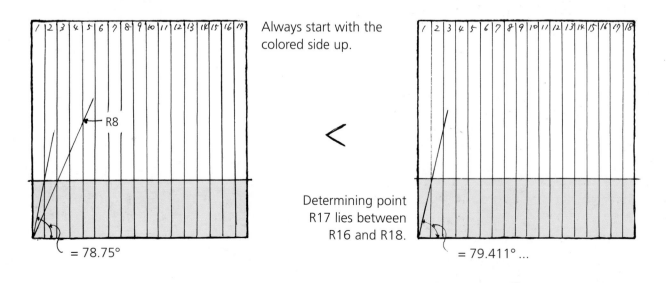

Always start with the colored side up.

Determining point R17 lies between R16 and R18.

= 78.75°

= 79.411° ...

Regular 18-Sided Polygon

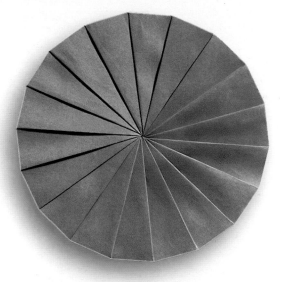

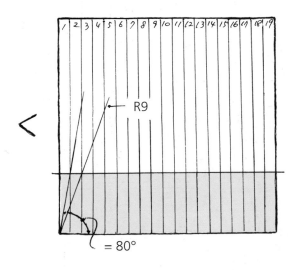

$= 80°$

It should be mentioned that in practice this folding technique has its limits somewhere between the regular 25-sided polygon and 30-sided polygon. (The latter in fact looks much like a circle.)

Since this folding technique always produces two regular polygons at one time, you may want to give one away as a present.

Regular 24-Sided to n-Sided Polygon

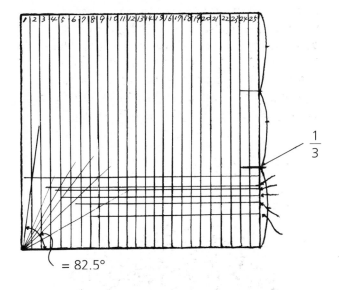

$= 82.5°$

As the number of angles of a regular n-sided polygon goes towards infinity, the n-sided polygon becomes a circle and the width to length ratio of the paper strip becomes $1/\pi$.

Two Theorems and Their Proofs

There are two important theorems relating to triangles: one by Euclid (4th to 3rd centuries B.C.) and one by Pythagoras. Both are necessary for the mathematics of origami, and both can easily be proven, using origami.

An origami proof has the distinct advantage of being instantly accessible and visible.

For all right triangles:
$a^2 + b^2 = c^2$ (Pythagorean theorem).

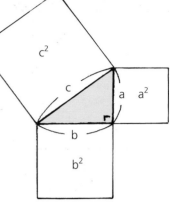

What is more, we can also deduce the following from figure A (page 43):

The total area of the square $(a + b)^2$ is made up of the two squares a^2 and b^2 and the four s triangles. Since $2s = ab$, it follows that:
$(a + b)^2 = a^2 + 2ab + b^2$.

In preparation for the proof, fold one of two equal squares as shown.

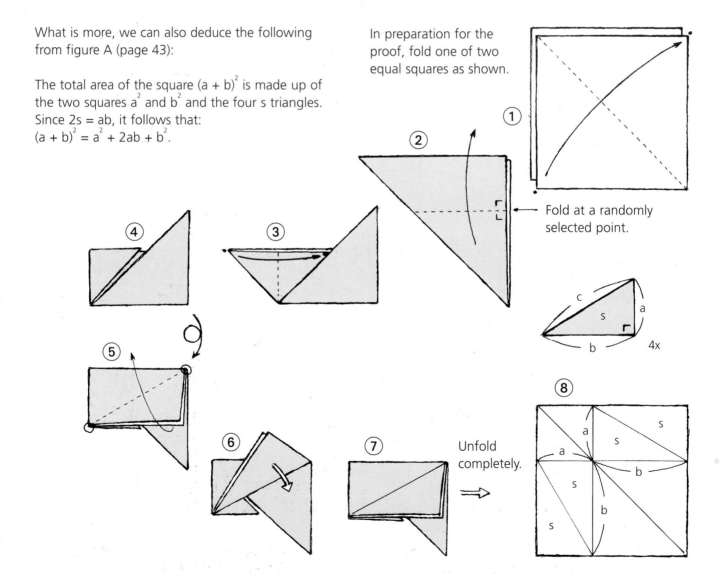

Fold at a randomly selected point.

Unfold completely.

For all right triangles, the sum of the interior angles equals two right angles:
angle a + angle b + angle c = 180°.

Three randomly cut paper triangles:

In I, II, and III, angles a, b, and c together form a straight line. It therefore follows:

a + b + c = 180° Euclidean theorem

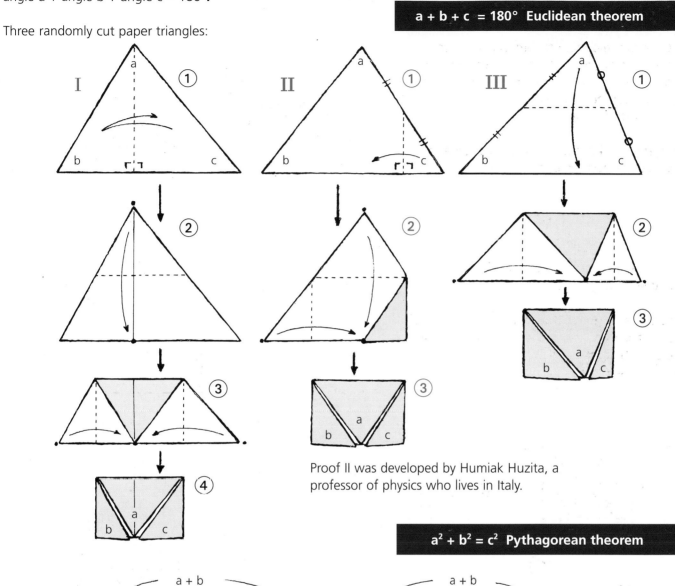

Proof II was developed by Humiak Huzita, a professor of physics who lives in Italy.

a² + b² = c² Pythagorean theorem

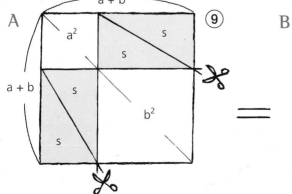

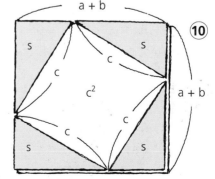

Now cut off the four s triangles and place them, as shown in figure 10, on the second paper square.

Since the two squares A and B are of equal size, the Pythagorean theorem has been proven.

The Super Tangram

The tangram was invented in China about 200 years ago. It is a puzzle that consists of a square that is divided into seven different pieces (see diagrams on pages 47 and 48). The goal is to assemble these pieces to form various shapes. You can also invent innumerable figures yourself; this is the reason the game has become so popular all over the world.

It is difficult enough to combine seven pieces in the right way — but we are playing with a Super Tangram made up of 20 pieces (see pages 44 and 45)! As an introduction, I have designed a few fairly simple puzzles. In addition to giving you the outline of the figure to be made, I have also indicated the number of tangram pieces required. All you have to do is to choose the correct pieces to cover the outlined area. (Hint: pieces may be flopped.)

You will see that even this is difficult. For this reason, I called my game "Super Tangram," the incredibly complicated tangram of the computer age.

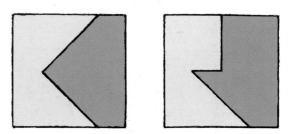

Tip: In the set of 20 blue pieces on pages 44 and 45, there are only two possible combinations for creating a square from two pieces, as shown above.

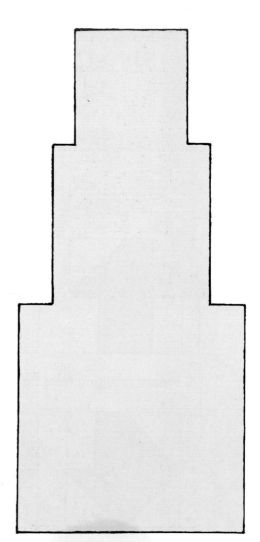

Puzzle 1
Use 14 pieces to create this column of three squares.

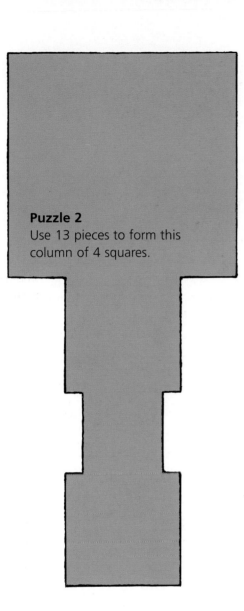

Puzzle 2
Use 13 pieces to form this column of 4 squares.

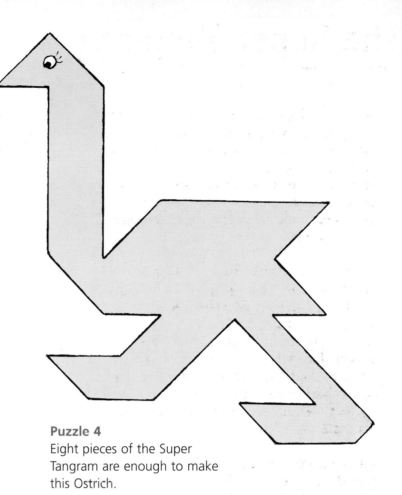

Puzzle 4
Eight pieces of the Super Tangram are enough to make this Ostrich.

Puzzle 3
Nine pieces make up this Swan.

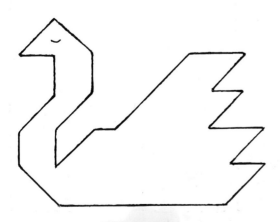

The most difficult task in Super Tangram is to assemble a square from 18 pieces. Mathematicians have searched for a solution, but were forced to give up. Nevertheless, it is not an un-solvable task; the correct solution does exist! But please, don't worry about this problem too much; enjoy the possibilities that origami opens up to you.

Origami and Tangrams

Puzzles such as tangrams and origami have one thing in common: their close link to mathematics and geometry. But the great thing about them is that they are not about solving difficult formulas. They are games, first and foremost, and are meant to be enjoyed. And more or less as a side effect we playfully broaden our mathematical, creative, and functional knowledge and understanding.

This is why I think of origami as the queen of puzzles, and I am sure that experts such as Froebel and Row would agree with me. In his work

Geometric Exercises in Paper Folding, first published in 1905, T. Sundara Row introduced a new tangram (see illustration below). There is only one task given here for this tangram, and the solution is not too difficult, but it shouldn't be entirely obvious how to form the original shape again, once the pieces have been jumbled up.

Why don't you give this version a try as well? Cut out the necessary pieces from cardboard. For their construction, see the diagrams at the bottom of the page.

Original Tangram

The surface of each tangram piece is 1/4, 1/8, or 1/16 of the area of the entire tangram.

Examples

Walking duck.

Running child.

Bow.

Row's Tangram (T. Sundara Row, 1905)

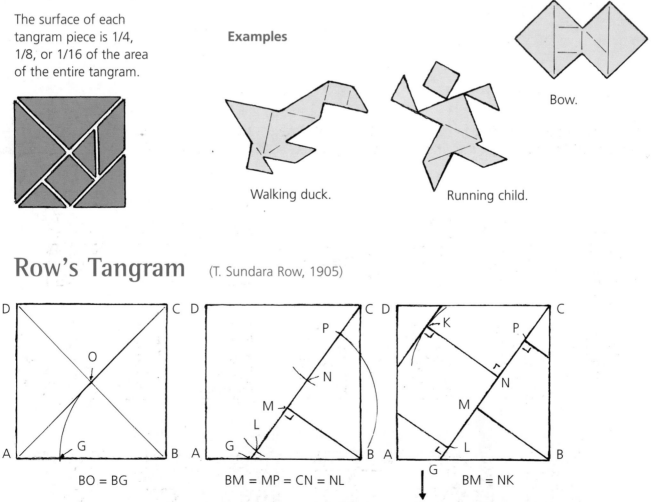

BO = BG

BM = MP = CN = NL

BM = NK

Puzzle: Use the 7 tangram pieces of the rightmost square to form three squares of equal size.

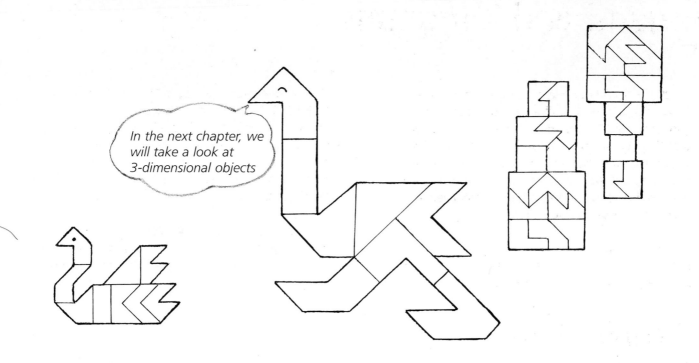

As you can see from the diagrams below, all 20 pieces of the Super Tangram can be formed from the elements of the original tangram. This proves once again that all 20 figures are equal in area.

3 Three-Dimensional Objects

Boxes

I am sure everybody will agree that boxes are one of the most popular shapes that can be made in traditional origami.

There is no limit to the shapes and possible variations of these. I would like to introduce a few in this chapter. The first example shows nesting boxes, a traditional model. It consists of a number of boxes of different sizes, which were all folded from the same size of paper. If you are wondering which box has the greatest volume, you can calculate this with the help of differential calculus, developed by Sir Isaac Newton (1643 – 1727), who was a physicist and mathematician. The box with a baseline-to-height ratio of 4:1 is the one with the greatest volume. If you need a more detailed explanation, please consult a math teacher.

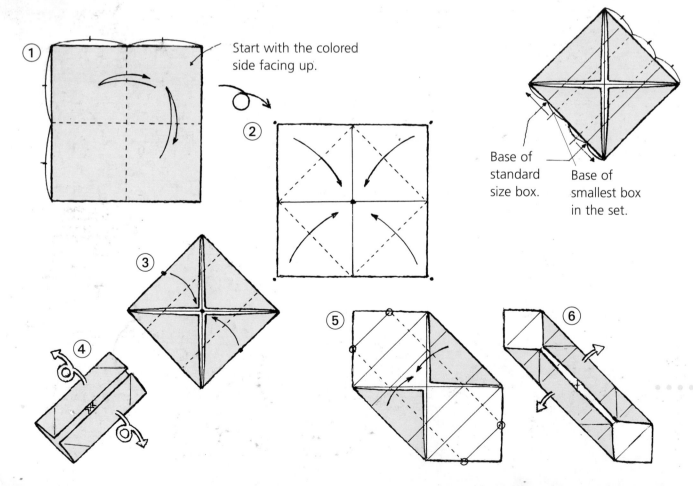

Start with the colored side facing up.

Base of standard size box.

Base of smallest box in the set.

Nesting Boxes

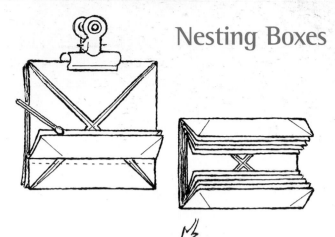

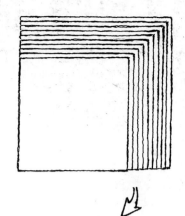

A

B

If you use the same size of paper for all the boxes in the set, and if you reduce the distance between the base lines by the width of a match's head (step 3), you will get the results shown in photo A.

If you use different-sized papers, the result will be as in photo B.

How about a game in which you mix the two sets of boxes (A and B) and then try to reassemble them in the correct order?

If you want a lid to go with the box, do not fold in quite as far as the center in step 2.

The simple box without lid is done.

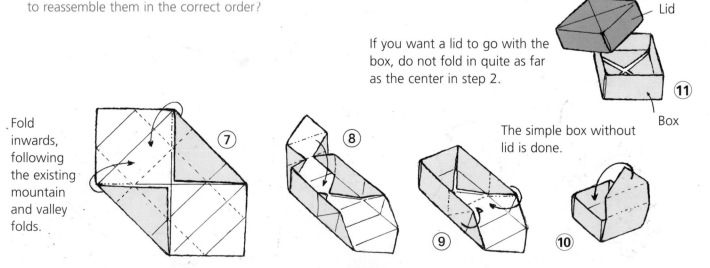

Fold inwards, following the existing mountain and valley folds.

⑦ ⑧ ⑨ ⑩ ⑪

Lid

Box

The Cube and Some Variations

You can make a simple cube by putting together two boxes that aren't quite finished (see figures 1 to 10). If you then fold one corner (or several) to the inside like an inverted pyramid (see figures 11 to 14), you can create new geometric shapes.

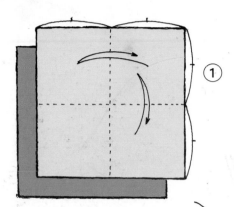

①

Use paper in two different colors. Always start with the colored side facing up.

②

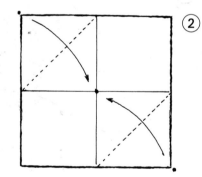

③   Mark.

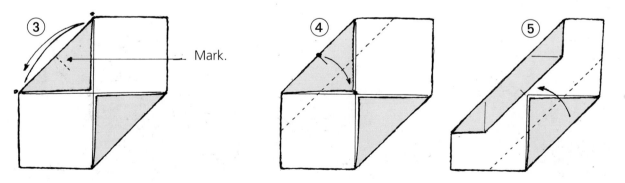

④

⑤

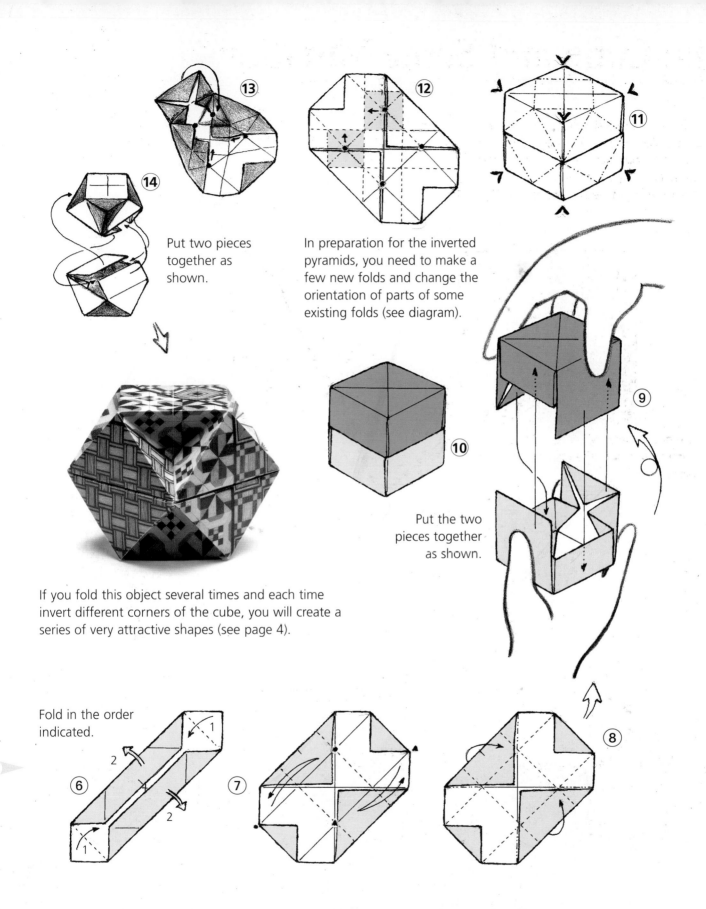

13

14

Put two pieces together as shown.

12

In preparation for the inverted pyramids, you need to make a few new folds and change the orientation of parts of some existing folds (see diagram).

11

10

9

Put the two pieces together as shown.

If you fold this object several times and each time invert different corners of the cube, you will create a series of very attractive shapes (see page 4).

Fold in the order indicated.

6

7

8

Regular Polyhedrons

The cube is a basic geometric figure, one of the five so-called Platonic solids or regular polyhedrons (*polyhedron* means "having many sides").

Which are the five regular polyhedrons? These solids are defined as follows: Their sides (faces) are all regular polygons of the same area, and each vertex (corner point) is the meeting point of an equal number of edges, which meet at the same angle. There are only five polyhedrons that meet these requirements. Three of them are composed of equilateral triangles, one is made of squares, and another is made of regular pentagons.

Best-known of these solids is the cube, which holds a great fascination for many people. A good example is the Rubik's Cube with its rotatable parts, which had people around the globe racking their brains for a solution.

The origami world is no different. Several hundred origami cubes with numerous distinctive features already exist, and more are being invented all the time.

You have already gotten to know one particular cube (page 53), but I would like to introduce you to three more variations, from a different perspective, and the other four regular solids. These five solids have a unique, indescribable magic.

Cube Made of Surface Modules

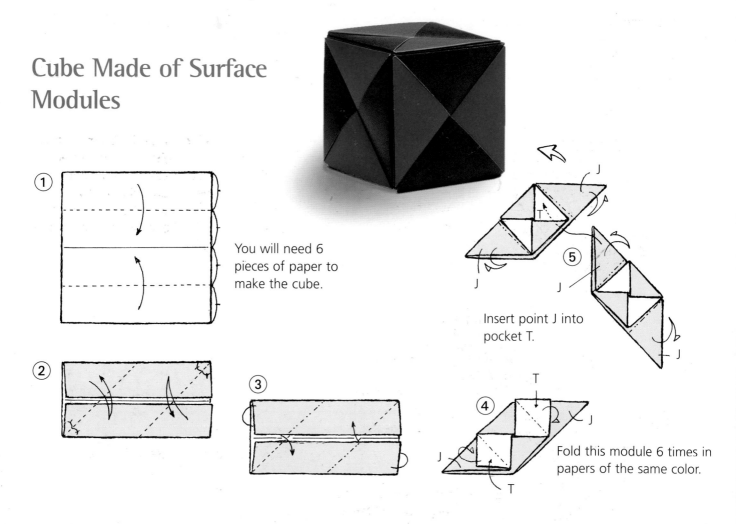

You will need 6 pieces of paper to make the cube.

Insert point J into pocket T.

Fold this module 6 times in papers of the same color.

The Five Platonic Solids (Regular Polyhedrons)

Tetrahedron

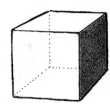
Cube

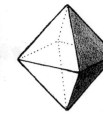
Octahedron

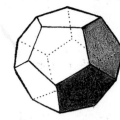
Dodecahedron

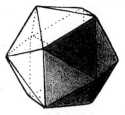
Icosahedron

Polyhedron	Shape of Side	Number of Sides	Number of Edges	Number of Vertices
Tetrahedron	Equilateral triangle	4	6	4
Cube (hexahedron)	Square	6	12	8
Octahedron	Equilateral triangle	8	12	6
Dodecahedron	Regular pentagon	12	30	20
Icosahedron	Equilateral triangle	20	30	12

Number of surfaces = 6 = number of surface modules.

The cube with solid-colored faces is also made from six surface modules. You might think that we are regressing technically, but these cubes are not about technique. Rather, I would like you to concentrate on the surfaces of the cube — one of its basic elements — the number of which corresponds to the number of modules used.

⑤

Make 2 of these modules in each of three different colors to make the cube above.

Follow the same folding technique up to Step 4.

For instructions on assembling the cube, see page 57.

Three Basic Elements of Polyhedrons

A polyhedron is defined by three basic elements, namely its surfaces (faces), edges, and vertices. Of course, we could also choose the center of a polyhedron's surfaces and the spatial center of the inside of the figure as the basis for its construction. But let's just stay with the three elements and the models that result from them, using the cube as an example.

Modules are closely connected with the solution of

our problem, because it is extremely difficult to fold a geometric solid from just one sheet of paper.

In order to simplify matters, we start by dividing the solid into equal parts, all of which correspond to a specific basic element (such as a surface). We then fold the required number of identical elements and assemble them to make the solid. These elements are called modules or units.

Cube Made of Corner Modules

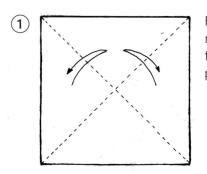

① Fold 8 corner modules from four sheets of paper.

A cube has eight corners, and it really only takes these eight modules to form a cube. However, for the solution pictured on these pages, six linking modules also are essential. In total, you will need seven squares of paper to construct this cube.

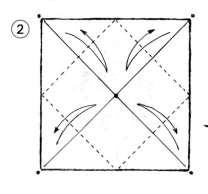

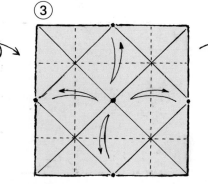

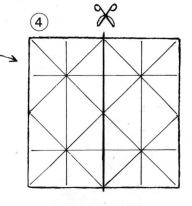

Cube from Surface Modules (continued from page 55)

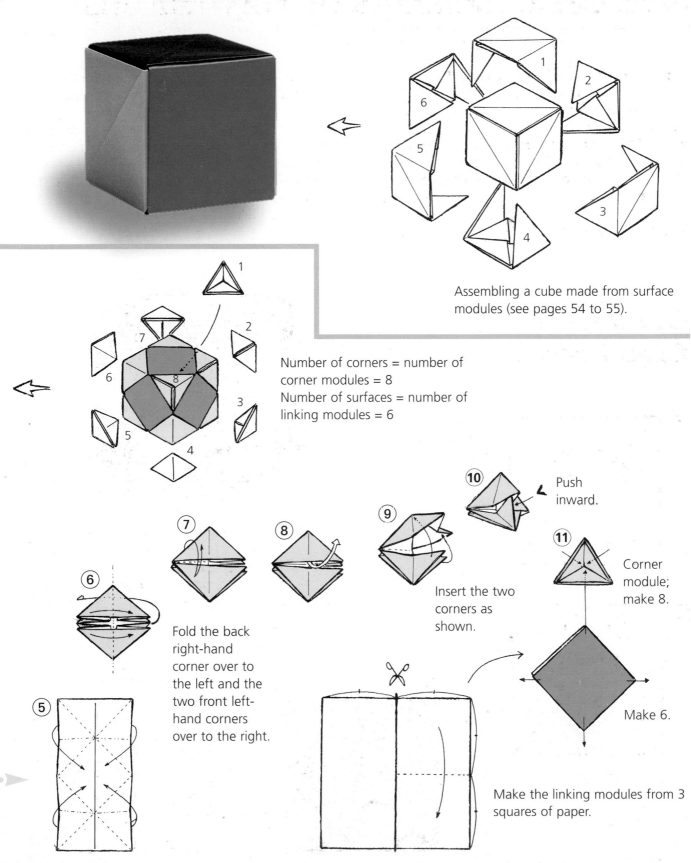

Assembling a cube made from surface modules (see pages 54 to 55).

Number of corners = number of corner modules = 8
Number of surfaces = number of linking modules = 6

Fold the back right-hand corner over to the left and the two front left-hand corners over to the right.

Insert the two corners as shown.

10 Push inward.

Corner module; make 8.

Make 6.

Make the linking modules from 3 squares of paper.

Cube Made of Edge Modules

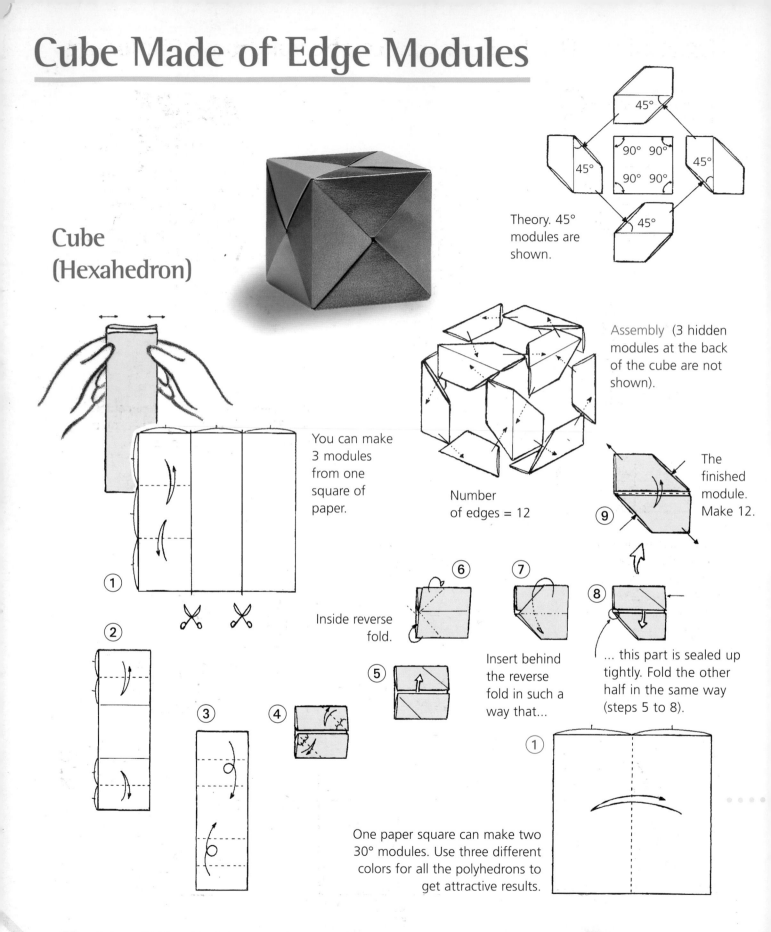

Cube (Hexahedron)

Theory. 45° modules are shown.

45° 90° 90° 45° 45° 90° 90° 45° 45°

You can make 3 modules from one square of paper.

Assembly (3 hidden modules at the back of the cube are not shown).

Number of edges = 12

The finished module. Make 12.

① ②

Inside reverse fold.

⑨

⑥ ⑦ ⑧

Insert behind the reverse fold in such a way that...

... this part is sealed up tightly. Fold the other half in the same way (steps 5 to 8).

⑤

③ ④

One paper square can make two 30° modules. Use three different colors for all the polyhedrons to get attractive results.

①

Tetrahedron, Octahedron, and Icosahedron from 30° Modules

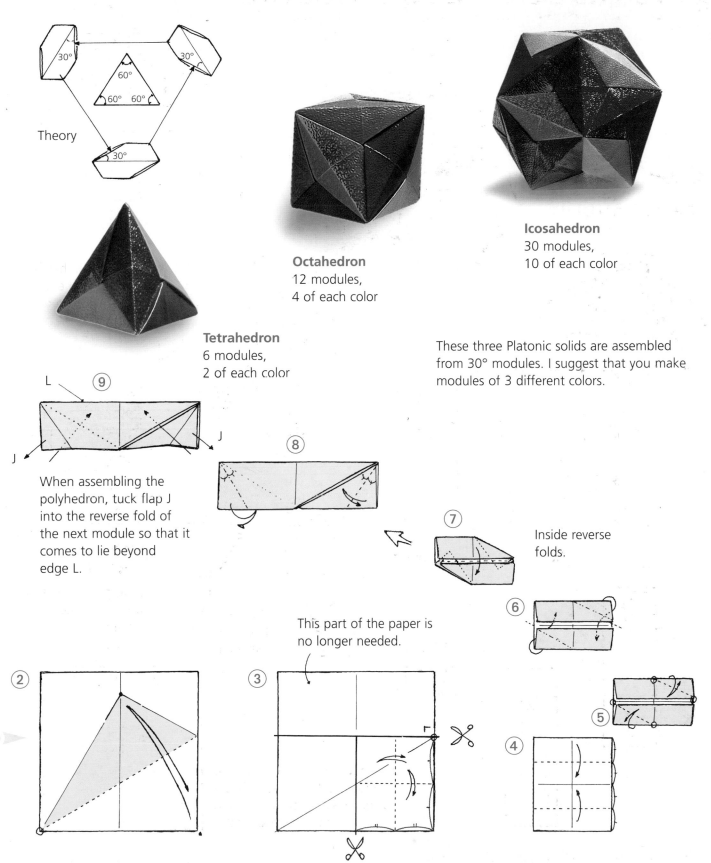

Theory

Tetrahedron
6 modules,
2 of each color

Octahedron
12 modules,
4 of each color

Icosahedron
30 modules,
10 of each color

These three Platonic solids are assembled from 30° modules. I suggest that you make modules of 3 different colors.

⑨

When assembling the polyhedron, tuck flap J into the reverse fold of the next module so that it comes to lie beyond edge L.

⑧

⑦ Inside reverse folds.

⑥

This part of the paper is no longer needed.

② ③ ⑤ ④

Dodecahedron from 54° Modules

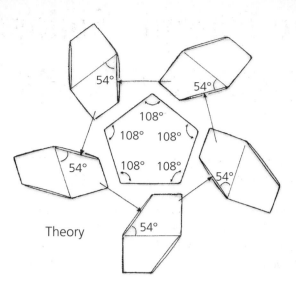

Theory

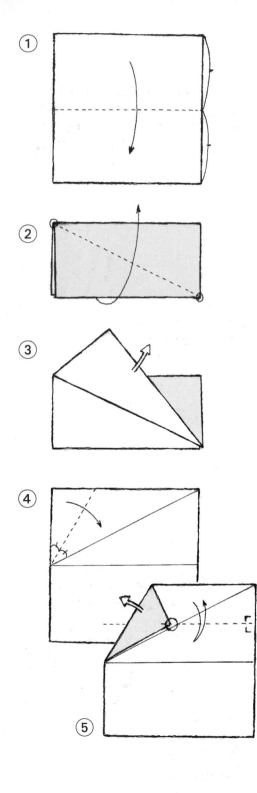

You can make three 54° modules from one square of paper. For this model, you will need 4 sheets of paper per color, and three different colors of paper. *Editor's comment:* It is possible to get 4 strips from one paper square; in that case, 3 sheets of paper per color will be enough.

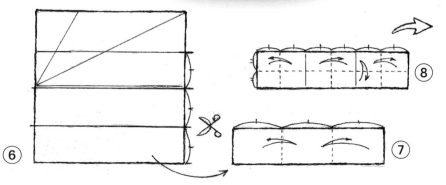

The Platonic Solids:
Five Good Friends

Now they are sitting before you: the five Platonic solids, including the cube made of edge modules and cubes of other modules. You only needed three different modules to make all of them: the 45° module, the 30° module, and the 54° module. All five solids were assembled in the same manner, and all five are composed of three colors each. This kind

of unified appearance exists only in origami. It wouldn't be wrong to call our solids good friends, something you will not find in any math textbook. And we can certainly continue in this sympathetic style and extend the circle of friends. You will find a few examples on the following pages.

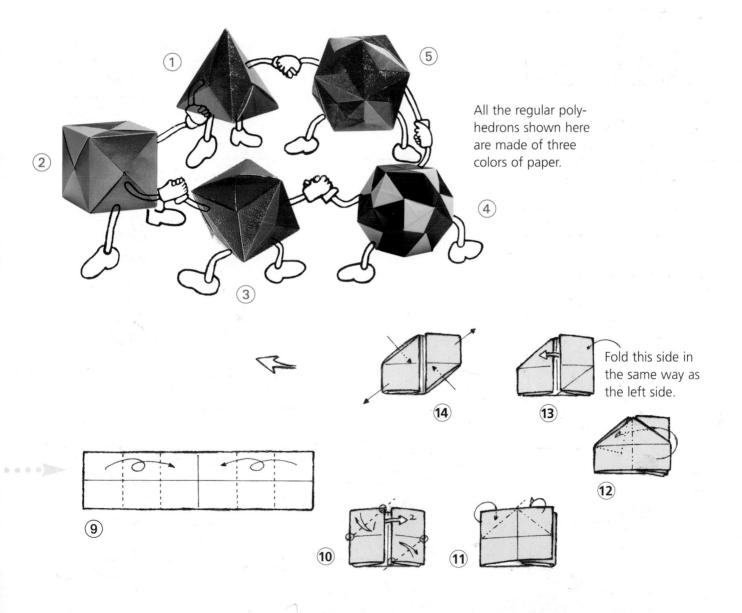

All the regular poly-hedrons shown here are made of three colors of paper.

Fold this side in the same way as the left side.

More Edge Modules

I have already presented one family of edge modules (45°, 30°, and 54° modules) in connection with a theory for the assembly of the five Platonic solids. However, there are many more variations on edge modules. I would like to demonstrate this with the example of the octahedron. In addition to the construction method I introduced previously (see model A), I will show you four more versions of an octahedron made from edge modules (see figures B, C, D and E). These edge modules can also be developed for the other polyhedrons, so that there is a total of 5 x 5 = 25 variations for these five polyhedrons.

Why not try to develop these edge modules yourself, and then go on to assemble a multitude of Platonic solids?

Incidentally, models B, C and E have been constructed starting from the spatial center.

The three-colored models B to E require four sheets of paper per color — a total of twelve sheets.

For models B and E, I recommend that you apply some glue to the connecting flap prior to assembly.

A

B

The finished B module. Make 12.

⑥

⑤

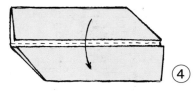
④

Inside reverse fold.

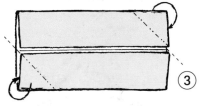
③

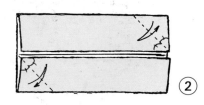
②

B

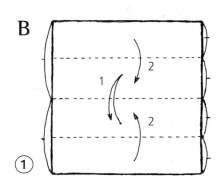
①

Fold in the order indicated.

The Octahedron: Five Variations

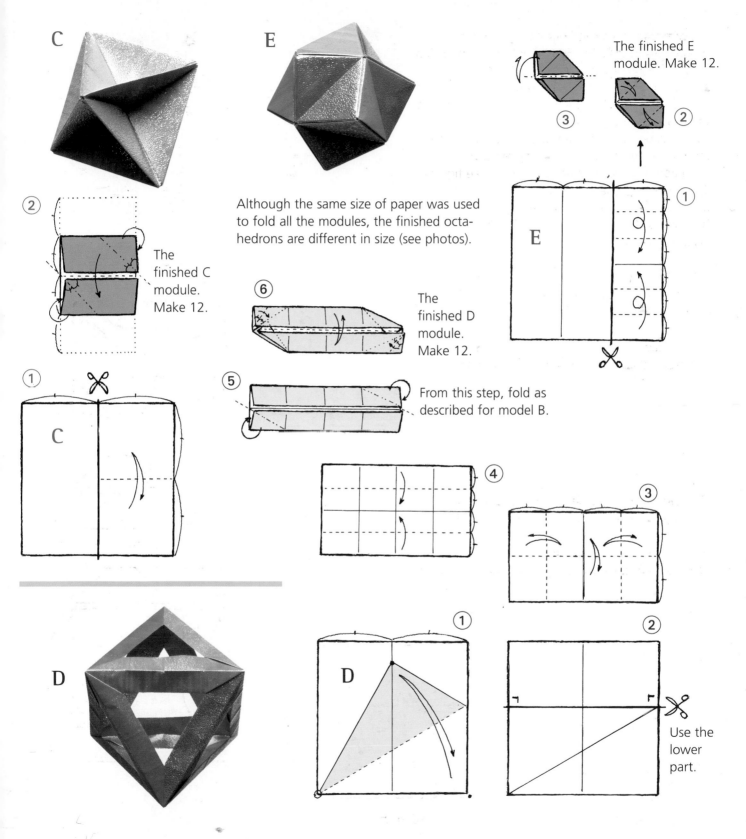

C

E

The finished E module. Make 12.

③ ②

Although the same size of paper was used to fold all the modules, the finished octahedrons are different in size (see photos).

② The finished C module. Make 12.

E ①

⑥ The finished D module. Make 12.

① C

⑤ From this step, fold as described for model B.

④

③

① D

② Use the lower part.

D

Afterword

For more than twenty years, I have been working with polyhedrons. They are central to my practicing origami. You may find this somewhat odd, and you may wonder why one person would want to spend so much time on five geometric figures. However, more than 2300 years ago in Greece, Euclid composed several volumes of teaching materials entitled *Stoicheia* (Elements), and to date, these too have lost none of their fascination. It is therefore hardly surprising that the main subject of Euclid's writing, the polyhedrons, have still got me in their grip.

With this book, I wanted to introduce you to the beauty and fascination of geometry and mathematics. To show you that there are numerous, almost unlimited possibilities for continuing this exciting journey, I would like to end with a little experiment: Pick up your completed five regular solids, one after the other, and turn each slowly. Observe how the shape of its outline changes. Take the cube, for instance: depending on how you turn it, you can see its outline as a square, a regular hexagon and finally a rectangle. You can make the same observations for the octahedron. What happens for the other three solids? Exploring the relationships between these five solids alone is very intriguing and leads you deep into the world of geometry.

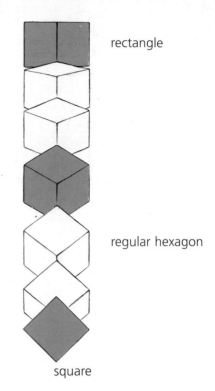

rectangle

regular hexagon

square

Index